The Blended Classroom
A Guide for Technology Supported Learning

By Kerry Rice

MOVING AT THE SPEED OF TECHNOLOGY

Blended Learning: The Basics

The latest buzz in educational circles is the "blended" classroom, but what does this mean in practical terms? And how is it different from more traditional forms of technology integration in the classroom? Traditional technology integration activities leverage technology for instruction but the basic structure of the classroom remains the same. Whereas a blended approach, leverages technology to restructure the classroom experience and repurpose the classroom space. The end goal is a more productive and efficient use of classroom time. In this guide, you'll explore the foundations of Blended Learning models, examine the potential opportunities for transforming your classroom and look at some of the tools and strategies best suited for the blended classroom.

Blended Learning is not just about adding a digital component to your classroom activities. It is about implementing what may be an entirely new model of teaching, where the focus is placed prominently on what is to be learned, rather than what is to be taught. It means rethinking the traditional classroom model, leveraging technology in a way that promotes more personalized learning and increases efficiencies in how precious classroom time is utilized. As you explore this guide and perhaps begin to visualize your new classroom space, keep the following in mind:

- Don't start with the technology. Begin with the problem you want your learning experience to solve.

- Use technology judiciously to support, enhance and differentiate instruction.

- Set concrete goals about what students will know and be able to do at the end of your instruction.

- Reference assessments at the beginning, middle and end of lesson preparation and delivery.

- Develop a plan and define your role in the process.

- Empower students to apply their knowledge in real world applications.

- Create shared spaces for collaboration and repositories of resources for sharing.

- Develop and plan across disciplines and grade levels.

- Critically reflect on practice thoughtfully and often.

The Blended Classroom Defined

When your learning environment shifts to blended, you will begin to make decisions about what aspects of the learning process are online, mobile, or are otherwise handled outside of normal class time and what aspects should be covered during the place-based classroom time. This reconfiguration of classroom time is at the heart of the blended classroom. It is not simply posting lectures online or providing resources for students to access at home - although this is certainly one aspect. It is about understanding how to make your classroom time, the time you spend with students, more productive and efficient. It is about freeing up time and space for more personalized learning opportunities, differentiating instruction and promoting hands-on, experiential activities.

WHAT IT IS AND HOW IT WORKS

Blended Learning refers to a mix of educational learning modalities, and can mean different things depending on context. Typically it will involve a mix between synchronous (real-time) and asynchronous (delayed-time) learning options, along with a mix of physical and online interactions. Many schools use learning management systems (LMS) such as Blackboard, Moodle, or Haiku, to support a Blended Learning experience for their students. However, it is quite achievable to create Blended Learning for a classroom without an LMS. For example, a teacher could integrate online communication options (such as IM, Skype, or web conferencing), along with access to online content using a blog or wiki to frame different learning activities. A formal definition of Blended Learning has been proposed by the Christensen Institute (formerly the Innosight Institute) (Straker & Horn, 2012):

> Blended Learning is a formal education program in which a student learns
> at least in part through online delivery of content and instruction with
> some element of student control over time, place, path and/or pace AND
> at least in part at a supervised brick-and-mortar location away from home.

This definition assumes that Blended Learning is formal education and should be distinguished from informal education. For example, students using the Internet or instructional software on their own, would not be considered Blended Learning in this context. A distinction is also made between Blended Learning and other types of technology rich environments. For example, online learning in the form of a full-time virtual school, may have some of the same characteristics as a blended environment but they differ in key ways. A full description of the four major categories of Blended Learning articulated by Straker and Horn (2012) is included below. For the purposes of this guide, we will focus primarily on strategy development in those sub-categories that fall under the Rotation Model since this is the model most closely associated with a traditional school environment where the majority of you will be based. However, this does not preclude the use of the strategies, described in this guide, in multiple types of blended environments.

5

BLENDED MODELS

Heather Straker and Michael Horn (2012) suggest some preliminary definitions and a framework of the models of Blended Learning environments. The main categories are at the program or school level, while their are several subcategories at the classroom level. Below is a brief overview of their blended model categorizations.

1. Rotation Model: Students rotate on a fixed schedule between learning modalities, one of which is online. This category includes four sub-categories:

   - Station Rotation - classroom-based stations in which whole-class, groups or individual students rotate. All students rotate through all stations.
   - Lab Rotation - campus-based stations in which whole-class, groups or individual students rotate. At least one lab is predominately online.
   - Flipped Classroom - students rotate between face-to-face guided practice in the classroom and online delivery of content from a remote location.
   - Individual Rotation - classroom-based stations in which students rotate based on individual need. Not all students will rotate through all stations.

2. Flex Model: Most content is delivered through the Internet or online and students move between online and face-to-face based on individual need. For example, the face-to-face interactions may include targeted interventions for tutoring or some kind of small group instruction or project.

3. Self-Blend Model: Students self-blend their curriculum by taking one or more courses completely online, through a supplemental program for example. The online courses *may* be supported by an on-site school lab.

4. Enriched Virtual Model: This is a modification of full-time virtual schools in which students divide their time, within a course, between online instruction and face-to-face instruction. Students may only meet during their first session, or periodically throughout the semester.

Although these models are useful for descriptive purposes, they should not define what your classroom looks like. And like all things technology related, they are changing all the time! Many schools and classrooms have successfully implemented Blended Learning following none of them, or following some of them in a combined mashup that fits with the needs of their school and their students. What they do provide is a framework for helping us understand what a true Blended Learning experience should encompass.

THE DIGITAL CLASSROOM VS. THE BLENDED CLASSROOM

This section could be retitled "No, you are not doing blended if..." because the vast majority of classrooms, even if they are technologically savvy, are what could be more accurately described as digital or technology rich classrooms. These classrooms may have access to a fully outfitted, state of the art technology lab. Could have access to mobile laptops and could even be one of the lucky few with one-to-one device initiatives. But integrating technology into the classroom, is very different than a blended classroom. Blending entails the acceptance of a new vision of teaching and learning. It is so much more about the teaching (and learning) than it is about the technology. So, you are **not** doing blended if...

- You have a class website with links to homework, practice quizzes, or other resources that supplement your instruction.
- Students use instructional software during class time or even after school for remediation.
- You incorporate WebQuests, Scavenger Hunts or other Internet-based activities into your normal classroom curriculum.
- You conduct after school chats using a Web-based chat tool, or you create video or recorded tutorials for struggling students.

Check out this great video, which explains in greater detail the important differences between Blended Learning and Technology Integration. The three key elements in Blended Learning that are important to remember are: 1) Allow flexibility in time, place and pace, 2) provide opportunities for frequent, on-demand assessments, and 3) embed multiple pathways to learning and mastery into the instruction. If you are interested in learning more about the developing Blended Learning framework and taxonomy, you are encouraged to visit the Christensen Institute website.

RESOURCES

- Blended Learning and Technology Integration (video): http://youtu.be/KD8AUfGsCKg
- 10 Benefits of Blended Learning for Teachers (infographic): http://bit.ly/1wYp1NO
- iNACOL Blended Learning Teacher Competency Framework: http://bit.ly/1B05HAV
- Intel Teach Elements Blended Learning Toolkit: http://intel.ly/1rvBW8V
- Edutopia, Five Minute Film Festival: The Basics of Blended Learning: http://bit.ly/1ECnUIG
- Teaching Channel: https://www.teachingchannel.org
- Blended Learning Toolkit: http://blended.online.ucf.edu

Learner-Centered Teaching

To help you better understand the concept of Blended Learning, this section provides some general methods for transitioning to a more personalized learning environment, regardless of subject matter. Think of this as wetting your appetite for what's to come. I encourage you to rid yourself of any pre-existing, and often culturally-embedded, ideas about education. It's true what they say - we tend to teach the way we were taught - simply because it's all we know. This is your chance to think outside the box. It's equally important to share what you learn with your colleagues and especially with your administration who often have the power to initiate the kind of change you will need to realize your vision - and which, if you are lucky, may be their vision as well! Be open, be creative, and above all keep student learning first and foremost in your mind.

As you begin this process of transition, caution should be taken not to throw the baby out with the bathwater, as it were. This notion of student-centered vs. teacher-directed instruction should be thought of as a continuum; not an either or. Moss (2002) suggests that by targeting the learning goals first, the levels of teacher directedness can then be varied to support learners' progress toward those goals. The trick is to figure out what combination of learner-centered and teacher-centered approaches produces the most effective *learning-centered* environment. Table 1 below provides simplified conceptual differences between teacher-centered and learner-centered strategies. Notice the passive role of learners in a teacher-centered environment.

Table 1. Teacher-centered vs. learner-centered strategies.

Teacher-Centered	Learner-Centered
Teacher-led discussion	Student-led discussion
Teacher assesses	Peer and self assessment
Teacher-led lecture	Teacher as designer of learning environments that support inquiry
Teacher covers content	Learner masters learning objectives
Discipline specific	Cross discipline and real world context aligned with learner interests
Structured and rigid classroom culture	Cooperative, collaborative and supportive culture
Assess for grade	Assess for learning
Students are learners	Everyone (including the teacher) is a learner

STUDENT ENGAGEMENT

At the heart of the discussion of learning-centered classrooms is shift in thinking about teaching practice. Simply put, learning-centered classrooms are based on student engagement in the learning process, not on delivery of information. This transition in thinking about teaching and learning is a critical element in the move to Blended Learning. And as a side note, Blended Learning aligns in remarkable and perhaps unexpected ways to some of the same tenets as the national Common Core State Standards. They both require a new way of thinking about teaching, about rigor, and about how well we prepare students to face the challenges of the 21st century. Both place students "*squarely at the center of the classroom, where they will grapple with challenging content individually and collaboratively, and where they will be expected to actively demonstrate their learning*" (Marzano & Toth, 2014). Understanding HOW to make the pedagogical shifts required to meet the demands of the 21st Century is critical to our students' future success. Inquiry-based instructional methods can provide a useful framework as we begin this process; they have the potential to increase student engagement and foster deep understanding of complex concepts through the use of hands-on, research-focused teaching and learning.

The Coalition of Essential Schools defines learner-centered teaching as pedagogy that "*acknowledges student voice as central to the learning experience for every learner and requires students to be active, responsible participants in their own learning.*" Inquiry-Based instruction is a learner-centered approach that emphasizes the process of learning and engages learners in investigating real world questions. It's an approach that provides a framework from which to extend and apply learning in a way that connects with learner interests within a broader thematic framework. In inquiry-based methods learners:

- Acquire and analyze information,
- develop and support propositions,
- provide solutions,
- design products that demonstrate thinking, and
- make learning visible.

Similarly, Project-Based Learning (PBL) is an inquiry-based teaching method that utilizes a project as a tool for investigation of a complex question, problem or challenge. The Buck Institute identifies the essential elements of:

- Significant content,
- 21st Century competencies,
- in-depth inquiry,
- driving questions,
- need to know,
- voice and choice,

- critique and revision, and
- public audience.

Inquiry-based methods have several advantages over traditional methods that rely on lecture and direct instruction to the exclusion of other approaches. Most importantly, they promote and encourage increased visibility of the learning process and outcomes to the broader community and they foster opportunities for differentiation; Two important goals of Blended Learning and the Common Core State Standards. With the addition of technology supports, the options for collaboration and differentiation are virtually unlimited. Below are just a few ideas to inspire you!

Collaboration

- Create a classroom **Dipity** digital timeline focused on a trend or topic and have students add to it each year. http://www.dipity.com
- Create a **Diigo** shared resource repository for your classroom. Allow students to join and share resources. https://www.diigo.com
- Post links to student projects on **Padlet** and ask students to post peer review results, or post the results of their brainstorming then arrange them by theme. http://padlet.com
- Create a class site using **Schoology**, a free learning management tool. Conduct online discussions and reflection activities. Add resources, assignments, videos, and tutorials for 24/7 access to learning materials. https://www.schoology.com
- Use **Google Docs** to share ideas or reflections. https://docs.google.com
- Let students create interest centers using **Google Sites** or **WikiSpaces**. Post a problem of the month based on interest. http://www.google.com/sites or https://www.wikispaces.com

Differentiation

- Create classroom books using **CAST Book Builder**. Embed the translation tool for multilingual students. Or better yet, let students create their own books! http://www.cast.org
- Create a free **WIX** website and post information using multiple representations as outlined by Universal Design for Learning (UDL) (i.e. text, video, images). http://www.wix.com
- Create a class discussion topic using **Voicethread**. Learners can respond in text, audio or video. http://voicethread.com
- Reinforce on-task behaviors using **Class Dojo**. http://www.classdojo.com
- Use **PowerMyLearning** to support differentiated learning with engaging, free activities on the Web. http://powermylearning.org

RESOURCES

- Coalition of Essential Schools: Learner-Centered Teaching: http://www.essentialschools.org
- Finding Balance: The Vices of our "Versus": http://bit.ly/1tmYnyl
- Buck Institute for Education: http://bie.org
- Edutopia: http://www.edutopia.org
- Introduction to Inquiry-Based Learning: http://www.teachinquiry.com
- 60 in 60 by Brandon Lutz: http://60in60.wikispaces.com
- Using Digital Tools for Differentiation: http://bit.ly/asdn2012
- CAST Universal Design for Learning: http://www.cast.org
- WebAIM (How accessible are your websites?): http://webaim.org

Literacy in the 21st Century

In its broadest sense, literacy is the mastery of language in both spoken and written forms. It is the ability to read and write. It is important to note however, that **every content area teacher is a teacher of literacy.** Every time a piece of text is shared in the classroom, literacy skills are being used and potentially developed to create meaning for students. It is imperative that content area teachers know and understand comprehension, vocabulary and writing strategies to further develop literacy skills for students.

CONTENT AREA LITERACY

Once again, the Common Core State Standards provide guidance on how we should proceed in content are literacy. Specifically, students should...

> **Comprehend as well as critique:** Students are engaged and open-minded—but discerning—readers and listeners. They work diligently to understand precisely what an author or speaker is saying, but they also question an author's or speaker's assumptions and premises and assess the veracity of claims and the soundness of reasoning.

> **Value evidence:** Students cite specific evidence when offering an oral or written interpretation of a text. They use relevant evidence when supporting their own points in writing and speaking, making their reasoning clear to the reader or listener, and they constructively evaluate others' use of evidence.

> **Use Technology and Digital Media Strategically and Capably:** Students employ technology thoughtfully to enhance their reading, writing, speaking, listening, and language use. They tailor their searches online to acquire useful information efficiently, and they integrate what they learn using technology with what they learn offline. They are familiar with the strengths and limitations of various technological tools and mediums and can select and use those best suited to their communication goals.

> **Build Strong Content Knowledge:** Students establish a base of knowledge across a wide range of subject matter by engaging with works of quality and substance. They become proficient in new areas through research and study. They read purposefully and listen attentively to gain both general knowledge and discipline-specific expertise. They refine and share their knowledge through writing and speaking.

Kosanovich, Reed, and Miller (2010) recommend the following strategies for content area teachers to help build literacy skills:

- Provide explicit instruction and supportive practice in effective comprehension strategies throughout the school day.
- Increase the amount and quality of open, sustained discussion of reading content.
- Set and maintain high standards for text, conversations, questions, and vocabulary.
- Increase students' motivation and engagement with reading.
- Teach essential content knowledge so that all students master critical concepts.

Guidelines are helpful, but how do they translate into practice, especially for the Science, History or Mathematics teacher? Below are just a few examples of literacy building activities that can be integrated into any content area.

Literacy Building Activities

Adapted from *Literacy as the Link: Common Core Standards and Content Area Teaching: http://bit.ly/SiN4W0*

- **Bell Ringers**: Assign short paragraphs from a textbook. Ask students to answer direct questions related to the text AND underline the evidence in the text that supports their answer. Gradually build to questions that require students to analyze, compare or infer.

- **Exit Slips**: Add text related questions to your existing routine. Question examples include: What conclusion from the text was supported by the activity we just completed? Which two facts most convincingly support the author's opinion?

- **Note-Taking Techniques**: Use a variety of media and organizational structures including graphic organizers, outlines, concept maps, and matrices.

- **Guess and Adjust**: Ask students to guess the definition of vocabulary based on background knowledge and adjust their understanding based on what they learned from the text.

- **Modify Text-Based Activities**: Use small groups, readalouds, excerpts, and highlight important text.

- **Connect Reading and Writing**: Base journal activities on excerpts or complete texts. For longer writing activities, require students to quote directly from the text.

DIGITAL LITERACY

"*Digital literacy is a critical 21st century skill. It comprises the end user's ability to critically evaluate digital content and to use that content in effective, responsible and ethical ways*" (Rice, 2012, p. 241). Because students don't always come to us with the requisite skills to master the Internet and other digital communications., it is important that digital literacy instruction be explicit and encompass the following:

- Evaluating material on the web
- Academic honesty

- Abiding by acceptable use policies
- Copyright and intellectual property
- Plagiarism
- Internet safety and privacy
- Digital communication
- Cyber bullying

Finding meaningful ways in which to leverage technology in preparing learners for the education and workforce demands of the future is also of primary concern to parents, educators, administrators and policy-makers alike. The U. S. College and Career Readiness standards propose that students should be able to:

- Use the Internet to produce, publish, interact and collaborate with others.
- Critically evaluate the advantages and disadvantages of various mediums depending on purpose.
- Integrate multiple sources of information in various formats and media to make decisions and solve problems.
- Evaluate the credibility and accuracy of sources of information.
- Use digital media strategically to share findings, reasoning and evidence.

There are numerous websites that can provide guidance on digital citizenship and digital literacy. Of particular interest is Creative Commons. Get in the habit of embedding copyright and intellectual property instruction into your lessons. Direct students to the free and easy-to-use copyright licensing at Creative Commons: http://creativecommons.org/. Dupli Checker is a free plagiarism detector: http://www.duplichecker.com/. Have students submit their own text for analysis before turning it in. Other resources are included below.

RESOURCES

- *Digital Literacy.Gov*: http://www.digitalliteracy.gov/
- *Partnership for 21st Century Skills*: http://www.p21.org/
- *Digiteen Project*: https://digiteen.wikispaces.com/
- *American Digital Library Association*: http://www.ala.org/advocacy/copyright
- *Plagiarism.org*: http://www.plagiarism.org/
- *iKeepSafe.org*: http://www.ikeepsafe.org/
- *Responsible Netizen.org*: http://www.responsiblenetizen.org/
- *5 Ways to Increase Digital Literacy via Blended Learning Models*: http://bit.ly/13P9aW2

Technology Supported Strategies

This section of the text is primarily a reference guide providing strategies aligned with best practices in Literacy for all content areas and Mathematics. A number of technology tools are suggested, but remember that first and foremost are the strategies that you intend to employ to facilitate flexibility in time, pace and place, and to make better use of classroom time. The technology tools can be substituted regardless of the strategy.

LITERACY, ENGLISH/LANGUAGE ARTS AND NON ENGLISH SUBJECT AREAS

Building Background Knowledge

Students learn best when they are given the opportunity to see, hear, and talk about subject matter before they are presented with a piece of text. This activates their schema (background knowledge) and provides a chance to build connections with the content.

Direct instruction or previewing...

Direct instruction on background knowledge can be embedded into an approach such as previewing, where students are presented with introductory material before they read text. It may include definitions of difficult vocabulary, translations of foreign phrases, and explanations of difficult concepts (Strangman & Hall, 2009).

- Record a video lecture

  - Screencast-o-matic
    http://www.screencast-o-matic.com/
  - Jing
    http://www.techsmith.com/jing.html
- Take a Virtual Field Trip

  - Google Lit Trips
    http://www.googlelittrips.com/
  - Smithsonian
    http://americanhistory.si.edu/exhibitions/
  - Virtual Field Trips: Why, Where & How-To
    http://www.internet4classrooms.com/vft.htm

Questions, cues, and advanced organizers...

Use questions, cues and advance organizers to help learners activate background knowledge and make sense of new information.

- Create a Mind Map

- Coggle
  https://coggle.it/
- Reflect and Record

  - Edublogs
    http://edublogs.org/
  - Vocaroo
    http://vocaroo.com/

Vocabulary building...

Vocabulary instruction is very important in helping students develop the academic vocabulary they will need as they move through subject areas in school.

- Build a Word Wall

  - Padlet
    http://padlet.com/
- Build a Word List

  - Vocabulary.com
    http://www.vocabulary.com/
- Create a Word Image

  - Wordle
    http://www.wordle.net/create
  - Tagxedo
    http://www.tagxedo.com/
  - ImageChef
    http://www.imagechef.com/

SPOTLIGHT STRATEGY

Semantic Feature Analysis: Semantic Feature analysis is a vocabulary activity in which the vocabulary is listed down the left hand of the column, and attributes or features are listed across the top. The students put a + or a − in each box to indicate if the vocabulary word has that particular feature. Learn more at All About Adolescent Literacy: http://www.adlit.org/strategies/22731/ Try these technology supports: Google Docs https://docs.google.com and Bubbl.us https://bubbl.us/

Comprehension

Have you ever had the experience of reading a book, coming to the end of the page, and realizing that you have no idea what you just read? This experience happens to many students, and unfortunately they lack the skills to monitor themselves and apply strategies to help them when they hit that perpetual rough spot. Explicitly teaching comprehension strategies give students the tools to better monitor and understand the text they are reading.

Summarize and take notes...
Ask students to identify essential elements in their own words, to reflect on their reading, or to pose critical questions.

- Journal and Reflect
  - Edublogs
    http://edublogs.org/
  - Vocaroo
    http://vocaroo.com/
  - Jing
    http://www.techsmith.com/jing.html
- Use Thinking Notes
  - Padlet
    http://padlet.com/

Multiple representations...
Reinforce concepts and vocabulary through graphic organizers, text, audio, and visual elements.

- Use Images
  - Clker
    http://www.clker.com/
  - Gimp
    http://www.gimp.org/
- Create a Graphic Organizer
  - Holt Interactive Graphic Organizer
    http://my.hrw.com/nsmedia/intgos/html/igo.htm
  - Gliffy
    http://www.gliffy.com/
- Use External Resources
  - Khan Academy
    https://www.khanacademy.org/
  - Phet Interactive Science Simulations
    http://phet.colorado.edu/
  - Best of History
    http://www.besthistorysites.net/

Identify similarities and differences...
Break complex concepts into similar and dissimilar characteristics for improved understanding.

- Compare and Contrast

- Diffen
  http://www.diffen.com/
- Compare and Contrast Map or Venn Diagram
  http://www.readwritethink.org/
• Create a Concept Map

  - Coggle
    https://coggle.it/
  - Bubbl.us
    https://bubbl.us/

SPOTLIGHT STRATEGY

Reciprocal Teaching: There are many strategies for scaffolding understanding of complex texts. Reciprocal Teaching is a small group strategy that helps with this process. Each member of the small group is assigned a specific role, generally: predicting, question generating, summarizing and clarifying. The group agrees on the amount of text to be read. Each member reads the text and takes notes according to the role they have been assigned. The group comes back together and each member discusses the text in terms of his/her role. Learn more at Reading Rockets: www.readingrockets.org/strategies/reciprocal teaching. Try these technology supports: Online Discussion Forums, Wikispaces or Google Sites and Evernote.

Writing

There are many reasons to have students write in the content area classroom and they may participate in any number of writing activities, including:

• Informative/explanatory text

• Opinions/arguments to support claims

• Narratives

• Research to build and present knowledge

However, it is important to recognized that students write to convey what they have learned, how they have synthesized information, and what new understandings they have constructed.

Convey what you have learned...

Provide options to encourage a broad range of writing skills and to motivate students to write.

• Animate it!

  - Powtoons
    http://www.powtoon.com/

- Create a Brochure or Book

    - ToonDoo
      http://www.toondoo.com/
    - PageFlip-Flap
      http://www.pageflip-flap.com/

Synthesize new information...

Use cloud-based resource repositories to facilitate storing, organizing and retrieving information.

- Build Research Skills

    - Diigo
      https://www.diigo.com/
    - Wolfram Alpha
      http://www.wolframalpha.com/
    - Google Related Searches
      http://bit.ly/1rEEyAP

Share new understandings...

Student created works should not be limited to teacher view only. Promote a supportive learning community by allowing students to share their work.

- Create a Collage

    - Glogster
      http://edu.glogster.com/
    - Pinterest
      http://www.pinterest.com/
    - ThingLink
      https://www.thinglink.com/

- Create a Presentation

    - Prezi
      http://prezi.com/
    - Google
      https://www.google.com
    - SllideShare
      http://www.slideshare.net/

- Create a Website

    - Google Sites
      https://sites.google.com/
    - Wix
      http://www.wix.com/

ALIGNING CONTENT WITH MATHEMATICAL PRACTICES

In this section, Mathematical Practices are explored and aligned with technology supported instructional strategies appropriate in Blended Learning environments. Don't forget, that Literacy is an important skill across all content areas – even Mathematics!

Make sense of problems and persevere in solving them...

Mathematically proficient students start by explaining to themselves the meaning of a problem and looking for entry points to its solution.

- Explore tools that support the collection, organization, and analysis of data

    - Wolfram Alpha:
      http://www.wolframalpha.com
    - Many Eyes:
      http://www-958.ibm.com
    - Microsoft Excel:
      http://office.microsoft.com/en-gb/excel/
- Practice displaying information graphically

    - Visual.ly:
      http://create.visual.ly/
    - Visualize Free:
      http://visualizefree.com/
- Use External Resources

    - Khan Academy:
      https://www.khanacademy.org/
    - Phet Interactive Science Simulations:
      http://phet.colorado.edu/

Reason Abstractly...

Mathematically proficient students are able to both decontextualize and contextualize quantitative relationships.

- Explore mathematical concepts

    - Tangle:
      http://worrydream.com/Tangle/
    - Online Discussions:
      http://edublogs.org/

- Probability Simulator:
  www.shodor.org/interactivate/activities/ExpProbability/

Construct viable arguments and critique the reasoning of others...

Mathematically proficient students make conjectures, thinking logically, reason inductively, create plausible arguments, and evaluate the arguments of others.

- Communicate with others

  - Online Discussions:
    http://edublogs.org/
  - Voicethread:
    http://voicethread.com/

- Use Thinking Notes

  - Padlet:
    http://padlet.com/

Model with mathematics...

Mathematically proficient students can apply the mathematics they learn, map mathematical relationships, and analyze those relationships to draw conclusions in the context of a given situation.

- Explore complex interactions

  - Tangle:
    http://worrydream.com/Tangle/
  - Number Pieces:
    www.mathlearningcenter.org/web-apps/number-pieces/
  - Geogebra
    http://www.geogebra.org/
  - National Library of Virtual Manipulatives:
    http://nlvm.usu.edu/en/nav/category_g_1_t_1.html
  - Model Algebra:
    www.mathplayground.com/AlgebraEquations.html

Use appropriate tools strategically...

Mathematically proficient students are familiar with tools appropriate for their grade, make sound decisions about when each of these tools might be helpful, and use tools to deepen their understanding.

- Make use of free online tools and apps

  - Interactive
    http://www.shodor.org/interactivate/activities/
  - Smart Protractor
    http://bit.ly/1qUKXrG
  - STEM on Mobile
    http://www.stemonmobile.com/
  - Web2.0 Calc
    http://web2.0calc.com/

- Conceptua
  https://www.conceptuamath.com/app/tool-library
- Core Math Tools
  www.nctm.org/resources/content.aspx?id=32702
- Calculator Soup
  http://www.calculatorsoup.com/

Look for and make use of structure...

Mathematically proficient students look closely to discern pattern or structure.

- Conduct a Survey

  - Google Forms, Spreadsheets, and Lucid Chart
    http://www.google.com/
  - Survey Monkey
    https://www.surveymonkey.com/
- Look for Patterns

  - Number Patterns
    http://mathforum.org/mathtools/tool.html?id=3031
  - Math Landing
    www.mathlanding.org/
  - Scientific Notation Problem Generator
    http://www.nyu.edu/pages/mathmol/txtbk2/scinot6.htm
  - Function Machine
    www.mathplayground.com/functionmachine.html

Look for and express regularity in repeated reasoning...

Mathematically proficient students look for general methods and shortcuts and continually evaluate their results.

- Collaborate and Share Results

  - Google Docs
    https://docs.google.com/
  - Creately
    http://creately.com/
  - Math Maps
    http://edte.ch/blog/maths-maps/
- Use Thinking Notes

  - Padlet
    http://padlet.com/
  - Creately
    http://creately.com/
- Test Hypotheses

  - Model Algebra
    www.mathplayground.com/AlgebraEquations.html

Attend to precision...

Mathematically proficient students communicate definitions, symbols, units of measure, calculations and their reasoning precisely to others.

- Build a Word List

    - Vocabulary.com
      http://www.vocabulary.com/
    - Math Glossary
      https://www.mathway.com/glossary

- Create a Word Image

    - Wordle
      http://www.wordle.net/create
    - Tagxedo
      http://www.tagxedo.com/
    - ImageChef
      http://www.imagechef.com/

- Practice Fluency

    - Learn Your Tables
      http://www.learnyourtables.co.uk/
    - PBS Math Games
      http://pbskids.org/cyberchase/math-games/

RESOURCES

Literacy

- A Blended Approach to Word Learning and Vocabulary: http://bit.ly/1D39LQ7
- 21 Digital Tools to Build Vocabulary: http://bit.ly/1oAFBQd
- Teaching that Makes Sense: http://www.ttms.org/
- All About Adolescent Literacy: http://bit.ly/1gGtEFS
- Background Knowledge: http://bit.ly/1nzfxVZ
- Cool Tools for 21st Century Learners: http://d97cooltools.blogspot.com.au/

Mathematics

- A Blended Learning Model for Math Instruction: http://bit.ly/1tvztgf
- The 36 Best Tools for Data Visualization:
  http://www.creativebloq.com/design-tools/data-visualization-712402
- Inside Mathematics: http://www.insidemathematics.org/index.php
- Which Blended Model is the Best for my Math Class? http://bit.ly/1D3lyOv
- PLUS Magazine: http://plus.maths.org/content/
- Math Leadership – Illustrating the Standards for Mathematical Practice: http://www.mathedleadership.org/ccss/itp/

A Phased Approach to Strategy Development

How do we get from this long list of strategies and tools to practical implementation in the classroom? This step is perhaps the most challenging of all and may require a phased approach, especially if you are not in an ideal situation in terms of computer access and school administrator buy-in. It can be very helpful to begin by searching the Internet for exemplary programs and classrooms. To assist you in getting started a few examples have been included in this section. Of course, the type of Blended Learning model or program presented here may not fit exactly to your own situation. But they can still be valuable in providing inspiration and ideas. The primary focus of this section however, is to provide you with explicit strategies that flow across a continuum of beginning (digital classroom) to advanced (blended) Blended Learning implementation.

BLENDED LEARNING IN ACTION

P.K. Yonge Developmental Research School
Blended Learning: Making it Work in Your Classroom by Edutopia

This is a good example of a one-to-one device implementation that uses technology to support and enhance instruction with a strong component of teacher directed instruction. The technology tools, at least in the case of the geometry class that is shown, are used to extend instructional time and to enhance conceptual understandings. Notice the time and practice it takes for the teacher to be able to do what she does effectively.

Akiba Academy of Dallas
Flipperentiated Instruction: How to Create the Customizable Classroom by Edutopia

Read how one teacher uses curated and original video to solve the challenging problem of differentiation. You might be interested in EdPuzzle - a video curation and creation tool - that lets you embed interactive assessments, along with narration into your own original video creations.

Aspire ERES Academy
https://www.youtube.com/watch?v=Zk7LMETFBDk

This program uses the Station Rotation model of Blended Learning. The video illustrates overall how students work in individual classrooms. Students rotate on a fixed schedule between working online and working in small group instruction.

Mont Hall V Middle School
https://www.youtube.com/watch?v=duAw-2mCbWo

In short this video, a teacher of Science shares her experiences with Blended Learning. Her statement that she feels "like she isn't teaching Science anymore, I feel like I teach students" is particularly interesting and insightful.

Nexus Academy
http://www.connectionsacademy.com/blended-learning.aspx

Nexus Academy is an offshoot of the Connections Academy fully online, charter school programs. This program combines both online and face-to-face courses with access to a physical location for targeted instruction. The college like settings promote positive interaction while allowing ultimate flexibility in scheduling.

Carpe Diem
http://www.carpediemaz.com/about

Carpe Diem is Blended Learning school, so this is not an example of an individual classroom implementation. But I think it is important to include here to illustrate how a system wide implementation can change the lives of students.

KIPP Empower Academy
http://www.kippla.org/approach/blended-learning.cfm

KIPP Academy is a particularly good example of a very successful, system-wide, Blended Learning implementation. KIPP Empower Academy uses a station rotation model to differentiate instruction.

A BLENDED LEARNING FRAMEWORK

The Blended classroom has received quite a bit of attention lately. Some see it as the solution to all of our educational problems but in reality it is just one more tool in our teacher toolbox to help us help students learn. But where to begin? If you are new to technology and Blended Learning in particular, or if you are still struggling with other challenges, for example student access to computers, you'll want to begin with strategies for the *Newbie*. Most of these strategies can be easily accommodated in a single classroom with minimal computer access. As you gain more experience and begin to understand and find solutions to the challenges, you can move forward to more complex strategies employed by *Explorers* and *Veterans*. Keep in mind, that the early strategies are not technically "blended" but they are often necessary in the journey you'll take as you begin to think transformatively about your teaching.

Tables 2 & 3 illustrate the continuum from Newbie to Veteran based on a single strategy for math and literacy, respectively. Each table includes information about the level of blending, the anticipated technology supports needed, an example of the strategy in action and suggested technology tools. For level one, the Newbie rank, it is expected that most of the instruction will occur during physical classroom time either as a whole group or in collaborative groups or centers, but the process is primarily teacher directed. Level 2, Explorers, begin to venture out of their comfort zone and may incorporate the use of rotation centers where some students are working independently while the teacher facilitates instruction in other areas of the class. Finally, the Level 3 Veterans have placed their instruction online in some form and the expectation is that learners will be working independently, at a time and place that makes sense for them, within the range of expected due dates or mastery learning. Learners may share their new knowledge or findings with the whole class in a physical space or online. None of the activities require the use of an LMS but one could certainly be used.

Table 2. Strategy: Explore Mathematical Terms

Blending Rank	Supports	Example	Tools
Newbie	3-5 classroom computers or personal device	Vocabulary practice using teacher created resources	Flippety Net Flash Card Machine
Explorer	3-5 classroom computers or personal device accessible at home	Use thinking notes to define and categorize terms independently	Padlet
Veteran	Personal device	Group consensus building online discussion. Groups share their findings with the whole class	Online Discussion Forum Google Docs Padlet

Table 3. Strategy: Build Background Knowledge

Blending	Supports	Example	Tools
Newbie	3-5 classroom computers or personal device	Whole class brainstorming	Bubbl.us
Explorer	3-5 classroom computers or personal device accessible at home	Read introductory text and reflect	Edublog
Veteran	Personal device	Independently reflect after viewing an online example presented by the teacher	Vocaroo Voicethread Online Discussion Forum

Table 4 provides numerous examples of technology uses for all content areas. Notice that a new column has been added called Technology Uses. This has been done to place less emphasis on the strategy in order to provide a more general illustration of the continuum, so it can be applied across a variety of content areas. For example, the first technology use, Internet Resources, may be applied as an instructional aid if learners were collaborating with classrooms outside of their school on a writing project or if the teacher implemented the use of online simulations or games. A shared resource repository would be useful if students were collecting information for a research report. Notice also that the supports have transitioned from a focus on the classroom, to a system-wide focus. This is an important consideration when implementing any technology rich learning environment. It can be challenging to accomplish if the system cannot support it. In some cases an LMS or Content Management System (CMS) is needed, especially as you move to the Veteran stage. This will be particularly true if you wish to use content from websites that are blocked by your school filtering software. This is when it can be handy to be in a school that supports your transformative teaching methods! I have not included links to all of the tools in this table. They can easily be searched on the Internet.

Table 4. Blended Learning Framework for All Content Areas

Blending	Technology Uses	Classroom Supports	Example	Tools
Newbie	Internet resources (Global Collaborations, Scavenger Hunts)	Computers, open access, bandwidth, asset or content management system	Collaborate in descriptive writing on a learning community or use virtual math manipulatives, simulations, games, tutorials, or tools for remediation.	Google Docs, Google Sites, Phet, Zoom Kitchen Chemistry, National Library of Virtual Manipulatives
Newbie	Shared resource repositories	Computers, open access, bandwidth	Preload Diigo with resources. Students use the annotation tool to highlight and explain structure and context of materials.	Diigo, CiteULike, Pinterest, Delicious, only2clicks, symbaloo

Blending	Technology Uses	Classroom Supports	Example	Tools
Newbie	Lecture Capture (for remediation or absent students)	Central LMS, CMS or class website	Record class lectures using a lecture capture tool. Upload to a central location for access when needed.	LMS (Blackboard, Moodle, Haiku, Brain Honey, Canvas), CMS (My Big Campus), or Website
Newbie	Classroom Website	Open access	Communicate with parents and/or post assignments	Google Groups, Yahoo Groups, Facebook, Blog, Wiki
Newbie	Collaborative Brainstorming	Computers, open access, bandwidth	Teacher directed collaborative brainstorming	Bubbl.us, Gliffy, Coggle, Padlet
Explorer	Internet Integration activities (WebQuests, Virtual Field Trips)	Computers, open access, bandwidth, small class sizes	Students work in small groups to complete a Webquest (Groups of students work in groups around a single computer.)	Google Sites, Google Forms, LMS, Virtual Field Trip websites
Explorer	Collaborative document creation	Computers, open access, bandwidth	Students work in small groups using online collaboration tools. (Students work at their own computer but belong to a group.)	Google Docs

Blending	Technology Uses	Classroom Supports	Example	Tools
Explorer	Online discussions	Computers, open access, bandwidth, microphone or headset	Practice language skills with others from the country of origin.	LMS, Voicethread, Skype, My Language Exchange
Veteran	Digital video resources (for delivery outside the classroom)	Computer access (one-to-one, after school labs, laptop checkout)	Khan Academy	YouTube, WatchKnow, TeacherTube
Veteran	Digital media creation	Computer access (one-to-one, after school labs, laptop checkout), microphone, Webcam	Teacher created videos explaining a complex concept using examples and materials from everyday life.	SnagIt, Jing, Camstudio, Camtasia, Screencast-O-Matic,
Veteran	Mobile Learning	Mobile device access	Situated Simulations that superimpose historical elements over real-time locations.	Smartphone, iPad,
Veteran	Gaming	Computer access (one-to-one, after school labs, laptop checkout)	Embed gaming elements into learning goals (badges, achievements, self-selection, leveling)	3-D GameLab quest-based learning management system, Mozilla Open Badges

As you can see, the list could go on and on. The examples presented are just a small representation of the possibilities and the continuum provides a framework and goal to work toward. Now, a good reflective exercise would be to take one technology use and align it with a strategy for your content area, then think of ways in which you could implement the strategy through the Newbie, Explorer and Veteran stages of transformation. For example, let's say I wanted my students to participate in a compare and contrast activity. Here are some steps to follow:

1. What do you want learners to do? Compare and contrast the characteristics of Apples and Oranges.

2. Why? Learners need to be able to compare and contrast treatments of the same topic in primary and secondary sources (CCSS.ELA-Literacy.RH.9-10-10-9).

3. Where and How?

   a. **Newbie:** Classroom. With direction from the teacher students will search the Internet for information and use an online or paper-based compare and contrast tool to construct their comparisons and discuss their findings in class.

   b. **Explorer:** Classroom and Home. With direction from the teacher students will search the Internet for information and use an online compare and contrast tool to construct their comparisons for homework, and share and discuss their findings in class.

   c. **Veteran:** Independently with Guidance. Students work independently to research and construct their compare and contrast charts and prepare a presentation (best if using audio or video) with their findings. They will share their presentations on the class Padlet site or an online discussion forum. Classmates will post a response to at least one other post addressing two components: "I like the fact that..." (complement) and "I wonder if..." (constructive criticism). Class time is used to clarify misunderstandings and to begin writing an essay.

Of course this is an extremely simplified example but it illustrates a couple of important points. First, notice that the lesson is entirely based on what learners need to be able to do. What the teacher will do is entirely driven by student needs. Second, the focus is first and foremost on the instruction. The technology is added in after the fact. And finally, when you get to the Veteran level, the amount of time needed for planning and preparation increases substantially. These are all critical elements in a successful Blended Learning implementation.

RESOURCES

- *Blended Learning Strategies for Engagement:* http://bit.ly/1HCuP2w
- *Blended Learning Toolkit - Student Success Strategies:* http://bit.ly/17eB3c7
- *Blended Learning Universe:* http://blendedlearning.org
- *Blended in Action - Video Profiles:* http://blendedlearning.org/directory/
- *Khan Academy Blended Learning MOOC:* http://bit.ly/14raOOr

Stray Thoughts...

A couple of items have been mentioned throughout this text that deserve some further consideration for those who are interested. Competency-based instruction (or mastery learning) is a concept that is becoming increasingly visible along with the movement to Blended Learning in mainstream education. In fact, as we begin to transition, ever more steadily to more personalized learning experiences, it is difficult to separate the two. The types of instructional models that align most closely with Blended Learning, inquiry- and experiential-based, are those that also align most closely with competency-based models of instruction. In a similar vein, and despite your feelings regarding their implementation, the Common Core State Standards also promote a movement to more personalized learning as well as a focus on college and career readiness. So let's take a look at both topics in this final section of the text.

COMPETENCY-BASED INSTRUCTION

Competency-based or mastery learning, although not a new concept, has until now, remained relatively obscure in U. S. public education. However, the emergence of Blended Learning, a focus on more personalized instruction, practices that encourage and promote more learner-centered approaches, and consistent and rigorous accountability requirements have all created an optimum scenario for a rise in activity surrounding this intriguing concept. It seems only natural that when we move away from the artificial structures of time, place and even grade levels, that our focus should gravitate toward student mastery of content along with acceptance that not all students will learn the same content in the same amount of time or in the same way. Competency-based instruction has a couple of really interesting features that make it such a good alignment with Blended Learning. First, in competency-based instruction we must be very clear about what it is that we want students to learn and second, when learning expectations are fixed, teachers and students need more flexibility in when and how they learn. Competency-based learning, like Blended Learning, is about putting learning first (as opposed to teaching), through personalization, differentiation, immediate interventions, flexible pacing and ubiquitous access to information. And technology plays a significant role in this revolution, for it is the affordances of technology that allow us to employ new methods at a scalable level.

Unfortunately, public policy has not always kept up with swift changes that technology has brought about. However, the success of several pilot schools and district initiatives across the country have propelled some states to action, primarily in removing barriers to allow more innovative approaches, such as competency education, to scale. For example, thirty-nine states have revised legislation to allow more flexibility for schools through actions such as seat-time waivers for graduation, acceptance of proficiency-based diplomas and credit flexibility. The best resource to learn more about Competency Education is the Competency Works collaborative project at http://www.competencyworks.org/.

A WORD ABOUT COMMON CORE STATE STANDARDS

The Common Core State Standards (CCSS) are much more than a set of content specific standards that students are expected to learn. They are most importantly dedicated to transforming teaching practice in a way that allows learners to develop those skills that will allow them to function in the 21st Century. Arguably the most significant national initiative in education since No Child Left Behind, the Common Core do not dictate how teachers should teach. What they do is articulate unified goals for literacy, mathematics and key 21st century skills. The BIG ideas surrounding the CCSS are this:

- All teachers are teachers of literacy.

- It is important to take time to unpack the standards and understand their intent and structure.

- The standards are not the curriculum; they are focused on outcomes.

- Important 21st Century Skills are embedded into the standards.

- Instead of asking: What will we teach and when should we teach it? Ask: Having learned key content, what will students be able to do with it?

Literacy

The Common Core is a shift in focus from what you might be familiar with in past standards. The primary emphasis is on a key conceptual change in thinking: The focus is not only on what is learned - as opposed to what is taught, but also a shift in focus to evidence-based, content-rich, reading and writing. These Instructional Shifts include:

- **Building knowledge through content-rich nonfiction.** The K-5 standards require a 50-50 balance between informational, content-rich nonfiction and literary reading. In the 6-12 standards, much greater attention is paid to literary nonfiction. Students should be able to independently build knowledge through reading and writing in history/social studies, science and technical subjects.

- **Reading, writing, and speaking grounded in evidence from text, both literary and informational texts.** The reading and writing standards place a high priority on the careful articulation of arguments, ideas and details based on text evidence. Students should be able to answer a range of text-dependent and inferential questions.

- **Regular practice with complex text and its academic language.** Building on the skills of reading and writing, the Standards address the growing complexity of the texts students must read to be ready for the demands of college and careers. Closely related is a focus on academic vocabulary.

Applying the Instructional Shifts doesn't mean abandoning methods that have been effective in the past. It just means thinking about them differently...

What to keep...

- Daily independent reading time.
- Ongoing reading assessments.
- Small group guided reading.

What to add...

- Opportunities for informal assessment.
- Reading conferences with monitoring and feedback.
- A 24/7 learning platform for online discussions and digital bulletin boards.
- Make "Why?" "How do you know?" and "Can you explain?" part of the classroom culture.
  - Guiding questions include:
  - Can you tell me what you read in your own words?
  - What was important about what you read? Why?
  - Why did the author state it that way?
  - Can you show me in the text where it made you think that?
  - Ample nonfiction texts at appropriate text complexity levels.
  - Language-rich classroom routines.
  - Cognitively complex activities that engage learners.

What to ditch...

- Student reading without monitoring or feedback.
- Fill in the blank worksheets.
- Uninspired lectures on information that students could easily discover for themselves

Mathematics

The CCSS for Mathematics are a challenging set of expectations for higher mathematics performance. They call for conceptual understanding, procedural skill, fluency, and problem solving. The new standards ask that the content knowledge and skills be connected in mathematical practice. The following instructional shifts are intended to help you meet this shift to greater focus and better coherence.

- **Focus strongly where the Standards focus.** The Standards call for a greater focus in mathematics. The content standards are significantly narrower and deeper than previous standards. Teachers focus on the major work in their respective grade level so that students gain strong foundations. The goal is solid conceptual understanding, high level of procedural skill and fluency, and the ability to apply math to solve problems in and out of the classroom. Know your standards and prioritize. Check out this quick guide: Grade Band Priorities http://bit.ly/1z686c0

- **Coherence:** Think across grades, and link to major topics within grades. The Standards are designed around coherent progressions from grade to grade. Careful connections are made across grades so that students build new understandings onto foundations built in previous years. Each standard is not a new event, but an extension of previous learning. Apply this principle by communicating across grade levels. This sample progress table will get you started: http://bit.ly/1z689V9

- **Rigor:** Require conceptual understanding, fluency, application, and deep understanding in major topics. Students are supported in their ability to access concepts from a number of perspectives so that math is seen as more than a set of discrete procedures. Students are supported in their procedural skill development (i.e. speed and accuracy) to facilitate access to more complex concepts and procedures. Finally, students are supported in the application of math in a variety of contexts, including related content areas such as science. Develop fluency using math games or programs. Sites like MathFactsPro can bring a fun element to math http://www.mathfactspro.com/. Aid in conceptual understanding using manipulatives like Geogebra at http://www.geogebra.org/. And involve other disciplines for real world application. See http://www.yummymath.com/ for math applications in real world scenarios.

The CCSS for Mathematics include both content and process standards. Content standards include the knowledge and skills students should learn, while the process standards address ways of thinking that students should engage in while learning mathematics. The content standards, what learners need to know, tend to be very straightforward, are specified by grade level and build on each other. While the Mathematical Practices are less clear, evolve and mature over time, and are aligned with cognitive development AND mathematical context. The Mathematical Practices represent the skills necessary for thinking about and interacting with mathematics in a meaningful and authentic way and they align with other 21st century skills for college and career readiness. These Mathematical Practices have been cited earlier in this text as a framework for the technology supported strategies but are addressed here again for convenience.

- Make sense of problems and persevere in solving them. Mathematically proficient students analyze, make conjectures, monitor, evaluate, explain and understand the approaches of others to solving complex problems and identify correspondences between different approaches.

- Reason abstractly and quantitatively. Mathematically proficient students are able to both decontextualize and contextualize quantitative relationships.

- Construct viable arguments and critique the reasoning of others. Mathematically proficient students make conjectures, thinking logically, reason inductively, create plausible arguments, and evaluate the arguments of others.

- Model with mathematics. Mathematically proficient students can apply the mathematics they learn, map mathematical relationships, and analyze those relationships to draw conclusions in the context of a given situation.

- Use appropriate tools strategically. Mathematically proficient students are familiar with tools appropriate for their grade, make sound decisions about when each of these tools might be helpful, and use tools to deepen their understanding.

- Look and make use of structure. Mathematically proficient students look closely to discern pattern or structure.

- Look for and express regularity in repeated reasoning. Mathematically proficient students look for general methods and shortcuts and continually evaluate their results.

- Attend to precision. Mathematically proficient students communicate definitions, symbols, units of measure, calculations and their reasoning precisely to others.

College and Career Readiness Standards

The College and Career Readiness Anchor Standards identify key skills that high school graduates should master to meet the rigorous demands of higher education and the workforce of the 21st Century. These anchor standards have been identified for Reading, Writing, Speaking and Listening, and Language. A major focus of the new standards is on essential reasoning and decision-making skills with an emphasis on higher order thinking and cognitively complex processing of information. Technology plays a role here as well. The Learning Sciences Marzano Center has identified critical instructional shifts in practice that are necessary to meet this challenge.

13 Essential Strategies for Achieving Rigor

The Learning Sciences Marzano Center suggests that the CCSS standards and instructional shifts require teachers "to plan not only what students should understand and be able to do by the end of the learning cycle, they need to scaffold their instruction from facts and details to robust generalizations and processes in order to reach these rigorous standards." These 13 essential strategies align with the goals of college and career readiness standards (Marzano & Toth, 2014).

- Identifying Critical Content
- Previewing New Content
- Organizing Students to Interact with Content
- Helping Students Process Content
- Helping Students Elaborate on Content
- Helping Students Record and Represent Knowledge
- Managing Response Rates with Tiered Questioning Techniques
- Reviewing Content
- Helping Students Practice Skills, Strategies, and Processes
- Helping Students Examine Similarities and Differences
- Helping Students Examine Their Reasoning
- Helping Students Revise Knowledge

- Helping Students Engage in Cognitively Complex Tasks

Students who meet the standards demonstrate independence, build strong content knowledge, respond to the varying demands of audience, task, purpose, and discipline, comprehend as well as critique, value evidence, and use technology and digital media strategically and capably.

Assessments

A complete understanding of the assessments that students and teachers will be held accountable to is an important step in the process of understanding the CCSS. The two primary assessment providers are:

- SBAC - Smarter-Balanced Assessment Consortium
  http://www.smarterbalanced.org/

- PARCC - Partnership for Assessment of Readiness for College and Career http://www.parcconline.org/

The CCSS assessments represent a change not only in what students will be required to know, but in the types of tasks they be asked to perform and the medium in which they will be assessed. The assessment are delivered online and are largely performance-based. Because of these changes it is critical that you become familiar with the assessments in order to judge the types of skills students will need to know just to be able to take the test. Visit the test sites and take some of the practice tests. As you do so, note the content being assessed and the skills and performances required to take the tests. Achieve offers a free toolkit for evaluating alignment of instructional and assessment materials with the common core: http://www.achieve.org/toolkit.

RESOURCES

- *Competency-Works:* http://www.competencyworks.org/about/competency-education/
- *Common Core State Standards Initiative:* http://www.corestandards.org/
- *Common Core Shifts in Language Arts/Literacy:* http://bit.ly/1gz8WaW
- *Applying the Instructional Shifts to the Teacher Practice:* http://bit.ly/1iqfUdQ
- *Standards for Mathematical Practice:* http://www.corestandards.org/Math/Practice/
- *Implementing the Mathematical Practice Standards:* http://mathpractices.edc.org/
- *Key Shifts in Mathematics:* http://bit.ly/1xMujuv
- *Scholastic - Common Core: Key Shifts in Mathematics:* http://bit.ly/1jHuAWL
- *College and Career Readiness/Anchor Standards:* http://bit.ly/1pwsxZE
- *Teaching for Rigor (Marzano Learning Center)* http://bit.ly/1hSgykd
- *The Inside Scoop on the PARCC and SBAC Assessments:* http://bit.ly/1CLoqRV

Transitions

I began this text as a simple guide for practicing teachers who were interested in implementing a new instructional approach in their classroom. And I end thinking a great deal myself about how education has both changed and stayed exactly the same over the course my life. I have been a classroom teacher and, trust me, have suffered through all sorts of new fangled teaching methods being thrust in my direction. So I understand the resistance, the frustration, the anger and despair of witnessing new method after new method pass by my classroom door. And some 15 years after I transitioned to higher education, I see we are still fighting the same battles. So the question is, how can we muster the energy to disentangle ourselves from the stranglehold of an outdated, impersonal, and yes, unforgivable (in terms of serving our students) educational system? I have to believe that this transition is inevitable - that students will demand it, that the advance of technology is relentless and that if we don't change, we will be left at the door with nothing but a bunch of empty desks because our students will have moved on to something better. The time for change is now and even the smallest change can have an impact. So hitch up your boots and get ready for the ride.

References

Common Core State Standards Initiative. (2010). Common Core State Standards Initiative. (2010).Common core state standards for English language arts and literacy in history/social studies, science, and technical subjects: Appendix A: Research Supporting Key Elements of the Standards; Glossary of Key Terms. Washington, DC: CCSSO & National Governors Association. Retrieved from http://www.corestandards.org/assets/Appendix_A.pdf.

Darling-Hammond, L., & Pecheone, R. (2010). Developing an internationally comparable balanced assessment system that supports high quality learning. Presented at the National Conference on Next Generation K-12 Assessment Systems, March 2010, Washington, D.C. http://www.k12center.org/rsc/pdf/Darling-HammondPechoneSystemModel.pdf

Kosanovich, M. L., Reed, D. K., & Miller, D. H. (2010). Bringing literacy strategies into content instruction: Professional learning for secondary-level teachers. Portsmouth, NH: RMC Research Corporation, Center on Instruction.

Marzano, R. J., & Toth, M. D. (2014). Teaching for rigor: A call for a critical instructional shift. Why essential shifts in instruction are necessary for teachers and students to succeed with college and career readiness standards. Learning Sciences Marzano Center Monograph. Retrieved from http://www.broward.k12.fl.us/talentdevelopment/news/teacher_links/Teaching-for-Rigor-20140318.pdf

Moss, C. M. (2002). Finding balance: The vices of our "versus". First Monday, 7(1-7). Retrieved from http://firstmonday.org/ojs/index.php/fm/article/view/924/846

Peha, S. (n.d.). Writing across the curriculum. Teaching that Makes Sense (TTMS). Retrieved from http://www.ttms.org/PDFs/06%20Writing%20Across%20the%20Curriculum%20v001%20%28Full%29.pdf

Rice, K. (2012). Making the move to K-12 online teaching: Research-based strategies and practices. Boston: Pearson Education.

Straker, H. & Horn, M. (2012). Classifying K-12 Blended Learning. Innosight Institute. Available: http://www.innosightinstitute.org/innosight/wp-content/uploads/2012/05/Classifying-K-12-blended-learning2.pdf

Strangman, N., & Hall, T. (2009). Background knowledge. National Center on Assessing the General Curriculum. Wakefield, MA: National Center on Accessible Instructional Materials. Retrieved from http://aim.cast.org/learn/historyarchive/backgroundpapers/background_knowledge#.U4e5pZRdXIc

Visit the associated symbaloo site for quick and easy access to the links referenced in this Technology Supported Literacy for the Blended Classroom Resource Guide...

http://www.symbaloo.com/mix/techsupportedstrategies

Made in the USA
Lexington, KY
14 July 2015